Matt Roberts

muscle up

A Dorling Kindersley Book

LONDON, NEW YORK, MUNICH,

MELBOURNE, and DELHI

This book is for my parents, John and Yvonne

Editors Michael Fullalove, Anna Fischel
Project Art Editors Paul Reid, Darren Bland for CobaltId
Managing Editor Gillian Roberts
Category Publisher Mary-Clare Jerram
Art Director Tracy Killick
DTP Designer Sonia Charbonnier
Production Controller Louise Daly
Photographer Russell Sadur

First published in Great Britain in 2003

by Dorling Kindersley Limited

80 Strand, London WC2R 0RL

A Penguin Company

4 6 8 10 9 7 5 3

Always consult your doctor before starting a fitness and/or
nutrition programme if you have any health concerns.

A CIP catalogue record for this book is available from The
British Library

ISBN 0 7513 4878 3

Colour reproduced by GRB, Italy

Printed and bound by Printer Trento, Italy

See our complete catalogue at www.dk.com

contents

about the book

At a guess, I'd say you're a pretty regular gym-goer, right? You train hard with weights, take trouble over what you eat, and yet somehow – you just can't quite figure out why – the body you're after is eluding you. Well, relax – you're not alone. Most of the guys who come to my gym for the first time say exactly that.

Building mass sounds as if it ought to be simple. But it isn't... until you know how. Once you've hit upon the right formula – and you're about to – building the body of your dreams becomes child's play. You might still have the occasional bit of fine-tuning to do, you'll certainly need to put in plenty of hard work, but when it comes down to it, you'll know the three 'ingredients' that are key to your success.

First up, it's the exercises. They've got to be right. For biceps that bulge and a chest that impresses, your muscles need 'overloading', 'traumatizing', literally 'tearing' apart. I've taken good care of that for you. In the two workouts that follow, you'll find 21 exercises that will test the muscles of your shoulders, chest, arms, and back to the max. With the right exercises under your belt, it's your technique

that matters. Good technique can make the difference between creating a body that's big and balanced and one that's strong but not necessarily the shape you're after. I'll give you my pointers for success. I'll also highlight the potential pitfalls to watch out for.

Last but not least, there's the business of nutrition. To help smooth the way for the essential 'muscle-rebuilding' process to take place, I'll tell you which foods to go for, how much of them to have... in short I'll show you how to eat yourself big.

Alongside all of this, I'll also be passing on the answers to those questions my clients ask me most and steering you through the murky world of supplements.

So grab your sports bag, fellas, and head for the gym. It's time to muscle up.

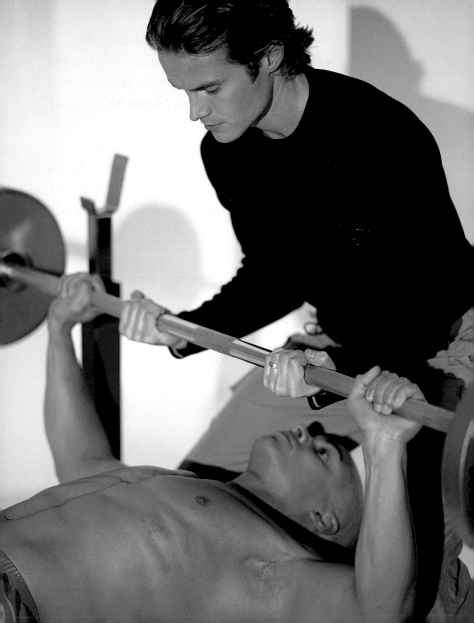

workout plan

Here's how you use the two workouts in this book

Frequency Aim to do each workout twice a week, performing them alternately. Never do the same workout twice in any one 48-hour period – have a day off in between.

Sets/reps For all but one exercise you're working on three sets.

- In the majority of cases I'll give you the number of reps to aim for. If you can't manage them all in the second and third sets, don't worry: keep the figure as your target to aim for. Once you can do them, however, it's time to put some more weight on.

- A fair few of the exercises involve 'drop sets'. In the first set you're aiming to use a weight you can do 6 reps with (say) and no more. (You might hear this called a 'maximal lift'.) You then drop the weight by 20% for the second set; and by another 20% for the third set. Drop sets can take a bit of getting right: if you find you can squeeze out more than about 10 reps in the third set, for instance, it means you haven't been lifting enough weight for the previous sets.

- On two or three occasions, I'll ask you to go for three sets of as many reps as you can manage in good form. The meaning of 'total fatigue' is then entirely up to you. The exercise that's the odd one out, by the way, is the concentration curl. You'll be doing a 'strip set' of these – it's like a drop set, but there are no rests.

Rep speed As a rule of thumb, allow 4–5 seconds per rep.

Rest times I'll indicate when to rest between sets and for how long.

workout one

The hard work is about to begin – on your pecs, your triceps, and the fronts and sides of your shoulders. I sometimes call this the 'push' routine.

warm-up

Before you start the exercises in workout one, you need to warm up for 5–10 minutes on a piece of CV kit. The rower or cross-trainer is best as they work your upper body as well as your legs. You're not looking to kill yourself here, but you should start to raise a sweat. If you decide to warm up on the cross-trainer, see page 52 for some guidelines.

on the rower

If you're warming up on the rower, keep an eye on your position. Your shoulders should be back, your chest forward, and your elbows in close to your body. A stroke rate of about 25–35 strokes per minute is ideal.

medicine ball throw

This warms your chest and shoulders through and develops power. Do three sets of 20 reps, with a 30-second rest between. When you get stronger, move further away from the wall.

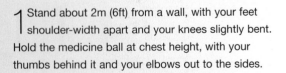

1 Stand about 2m (6ft) from a wall, with your feet shoulder-width apart and your knees slightly bent. Hold the medicine ball at chest height, with your thumbs behind it and your elbows out to the sides.

2 Throw the ball at the wall explosively, extending your arms straight out at chest height. Catch the ball quickly and pull it into your chest ready for the next rep.

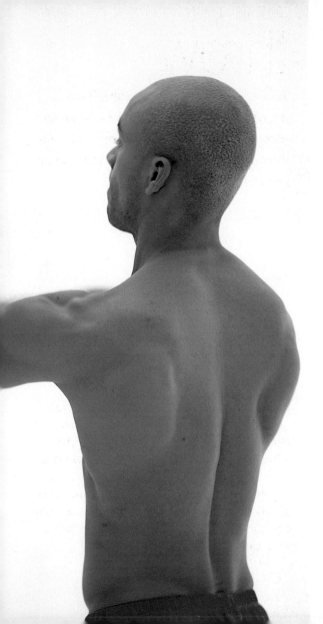

do it right

breathing correctly

The correct breathing pattern is all-important to your success in strength training. A lot of guys tend to hold their breath when they first start lifting – something that's best avoided, not least because it can send your blood pressure soaring. Get into the habit of breathing with the effort, so exhale on the up, and inhale on the down.

flat bench press

The biggest exercise first. Shift as much weight as you can here: you should be able to push out 6 reps for the first set and no more. Rest for 90–120 seconds, drop the weight slightly and do 8 reps. Rest again, drop the weight again, then push out as many reps as you can (aim for 10).

1 Lie back on the bench, feet flat on the floor. Squeeze your shoulder blades together (so you use your chest muscles correctly and don't overdevelop your shoulders). Lift the weight off the rack and place it over the midline of your chest.

2 Slowly lower the weight until your elbows are at 90° and the bar is just above your chest. Keep your back flat. Slowly raise the weight again. Watch you don't bounce it off your chest.

getting results

How long will it be before I see results?

Don't expect results straightaway. If you're fairly new to lifting, you will make rapid gains in 'strength'. This is not actually a result of your muscles becoming stronger as such. It's more to do with your muscles – and your brain – getting used to the exercises and performing them more efficiently, which gives the illusion of increased strength. Your muscles will then start to become stronger, and – after 8–12 weeks – they'll start to grow.

I'm trying to lose a bit of weight *and* build muscle at the same time. Is there anything special I should do?

You've got a bit of a catch-22 there. If the body is building tissue, it's said to be *anabolic*; if it's losing it, *catabolic*. It isn't easy to do both at the same time. You'll need to periodize your goals to a certain extent: I would suggest a 12-week muscle-building block with little or no cardio work (apart from warming up) to lay down lean tissue. Then, a second 12-week block in which you'll cut back on the weights and incorporate some long bouts of low-intensity cardio work such as cycling or swimming. You will lose some muscle size, but you'll also dump some fat. You'll get your leaner, more ripped appearance in the end; it just might take a little time.

I do loads of bench presses, but my chest still doesn't look that well-developed. Where am I going wrong?

Bench pressing alone will never give you the physique you're after. Although it's a pretty 'big' exercise that's great for your chest, triceps, and shoulders, it doesn't work all your upper body musculature. In fact, worse, it actually leaves areas of it unworked. Stick to the two routines in this book. Exercises like the pec fly are designed to work your chest laterally; the incline presses will develop your upper chest; in short, all the exercises will ensure you build the big and balanced body you're after.

incline press

Another biggie. This hits the upper chest and brings in more of your shoulder muscles. Work on three sets again (6 reps, 8 reps, then as many as you can). Rest for 90–120 seconds between sets and drop the weight with each set.

1 Raise the angle of the bench to 45°. Lie back, keeping your feet flat on the floor. With arms out at shoulder level and elbows bent at 90°, hold a weight in each hand.

2 Raise your arms until they're almost fully extended above your head. Keep your body still and back straight. Slowly return to the start.

dumbbell press

Into the shoulders now. Use the same set/rep/rest routine as for the previous two exercises.

1 Sit upright on the bench. Pull your abs in tight and grab the weights. Hold them out at shoulder height.

2 Push the weights above your head, extending your arms almost fully. Pause slightly, then return to the start.

When you're working your muscles to the max, your body needs water, whether you're sweating hard or not. Get into the habit of having a slug every few minutes. And be prepared to get through half a litre or more during every workout.

pec fly

Now for some isolation work, starting with your chest. Find a weight you can just manage 15 reps with. Stay with it for a second and a third set of 15 reps (but don't worry if you can manage only 8–12). Take a 60-second rest between sets.

1 Lie back on the bench, with your feet flat on the floor. Holding a weight in each hand, extend your arms away from your sides until your elbows are out at 90°.

2 Slowly raise the weights until your arms are nearly fully extended above your chest. Flex your pecs, then slowly return to the start.

don't arch your lower back

side raise

Some work now for the front and back of your shoulders and part of your triceps. Go for three sets of 15 reps. Rests are 60 seconds.

legs relaxed (don't lock your knees)

1 Stand with your feet hip-width apart and your knees slightly bent. Start with your hands together in front of you, palms facing each other. Pull your abs in tight.

palm facing downwards

2 Keeping your elbows slightly bent, slowly raise your arms to shoulder level. Keep your torso still. Slowly return to the starting position.

31

fuelling up

What's the perfect pre-workout meal?

Pre-workout you want something that isn't going to interfere with your ability to train. For that very reason, steer clear of heavy proteins and fats (which will only sit in your stomach doing their level best to reappear during the session). Most guys can normally stomach a carbohydrate sports drink and/or a banana before they work out, but experiment with what you can and cannot have. It's what you have straight after your routine that's far more important anyway (see below).

I know you're meant to eat straight after a workout, but I just can't face food then. Is there any way round this?

You're not alone – food's the last thing on most people's minds straight after a workout. And yet – you're right – it's just what's needed to replenish the glycogen energy supplies you've used up in your muscles. There's a 'golden window' of about 15 minutes post-workout when your muscles will literally suck up any carbohydrates you give them. It's where a good recovery sports drink comes in if you can't face eating. Look for those that contain some protein: they've been shown to have a recuperative effect post-workout.

I find I get really hungry between meals when I'm strength training. What can I snack on that won't sabotage all my hard work in the gym?

Go for fruit every time, especially orchard fruits like apples and pears. Almonds, brazil nuts, raisins, and pumpkin seeds are good too, as are the sunflower seed and sesame seed mixes you can buy in packets. But steer well clear of foods that are high in fats and refined sugars – they might satisfy you at the time, but will just leave your body craving more.

What changes can I make to my diet to help me bulk up?

You don't need huge amounts of food to gain mass: about 500 extra calories a day should do it. Make sure you eat a good balanced diet, with plenty of quality unrefined carbohydrates, such as wild rice, wholemeal pasta, and wholemeal bread, to provide slow-burn energy. Keep your fat intake sensible. And eat quality protein (but don't go overboard on this by taking powders and the like). Tuna, chicken, and beans are ideal. You can find out the amount of protein and carbohydrate you should be having each day on pages 65 and 73.

press

This works your triceps all the harder because they're elongated even in the start position. Work on three sets of 15 reps with 60-second rests between.

1 Lie back on the bench, with your feet flat on the floor. Hold the weights by your head, elbows pointing at the ceiling.

2 Keeping your upper arms still, slowly extend your forearms until your arms are nearly straight and the weights are above your head. Don't arch your back. Slowly return to the start.

do it right

two golden rules

There are two golden rules to strength training in my book. To avoid injury – and for the best results – keep them in mind at all times.

• Never work the same muscle group within a 48-hour period: always take a day off between sessions. Do some other form of training then, if you like.

• Never increase the intensity (ie the weight and number of reps) by more than 10% in a week. Take it nice and slow and steady. Your patience will be rewarded, I promise you.

front raise

A great exercise for improving the muscle definition at the front of your shoulders and your arms. Work on three sets of 15 reps with 60-second rests between.

elbows slightly bent

overhand grip

1 Stand with your feet hip-width apart, your knees slightly bent, and your back straight. Hold the weights in front of your thighs.

2 Keeping your elbows slightly bent, raise the weights to shoulder height in front of you. Maintain a strong upright position, but watch you don't curve your lower back. Slowly return to the start.

You'll be fairly ruined by now,

so give your muscles a bit

of a stretch to revive them:

we've got two more exercises

to push out to take them

to total fatigue.

press-up

Familiar but excellent work for your pecs, deltoids, and triceps. Go for three sets of as many reps as you can manage in good form. Take 30-second breathers between sets.

1 Place your hands directly under your shoulders (or slightly wider if you want to put more emphasis on your chest). Keep your torso and legs straight.

fingers splayed to spread your bodyweight

2 Lower your body, bending your arms to about 90° and keeping your head in line with your spine. Keep your stomach and thigh muscles tight to keep your legs straight. Push yourself slowly back up to the start position.

bottom in line with body
(don't stick it in the air)

triceps bench dip

This concentrates the work on your triceps. Again, go for three sets of as many reps as you can manage in good form and take 30-second rests between sets.

1 Sit on the edge of the bench with your thumbs at the sides of your thighs. Plant your feet hip-width apart in front of you. Keeping your back straight and close to the bench, move your body forwards.

feet hip-width apart

2 Lower yourself down, keeping your elbows straight behind you, until your arms are bent at 90°. Slowly push yourself up until your arms are straight, but not locked.

abs pulled in tight

stretches

Stretching may well be the last thing on your mind right now, but 5 minutes' work will keep you supple and ward off nagging problems. Do the seven moves in order.

1 chest stretch

Stand with feet hip-width apart. Hold your abs tight, but relax your head, neck, and shoulders. Keeping your back straight, clasp your hands behind you and lift your arms until you feel a stretch across your chest. Hold for 10–15 seconds.

2 bicep and chest stretch

Stand at arm's length from a pole or wall with the palm of your hand resting against it. Keeping your arm straight, gently rotate your body away from your hand so you feel the stretch in your chest and arm. Hold for 15 seconds, then repeat with your other arm.

3 upper back stretch

Stand at arm's length from a pole, feet hip-width apart. Extend your arms in front of you and clasp the pole, lowering your head as you do so. Keep your lower back firm and your torso upright. Hold for 10 seconds.

4 tricep stretch

Stand with feet hip-width apart. Raise one arm and place the hand over your back as if you were reaching down your spine. Gently push the elbow back with your other hand. Hold for 10 seconds, then repeat with your other arm.

5 shoulder stretch

Stand with your feet hip-width apart. Bend one arm slightly and stretch it across your body. Place your other hand on the upper arm to push the stretch a little further. Feel it in the back of your shoulder. Hold for 10 seconds, then repeat with your other arm.

7 forearm stretch

Sit or stand up straight. Extend one arm in front of you, elbow straight, palm facing forwards. Gently pull the fingers back with your other hand. Feel the stretch in your forearm. Hold for 10 seconds, then repeat with your other hand.

6 neck stretch

Sit upright with shoulders relaxed. Cradle your head with one hand and gently pull it towards your shoulder. Feel the stretch at the side of your neck. Hold for 10 seconds, then repeat with your other hand.

workout worries

I can feel my biceps growing, but can't see much change to my elbows and forearms. Are they going to end up looking all spindly?

Rather than working one muscle in isolation, most of the exercises in this book work your muscles through a full range of motion, and from one joint to the next. So you're working your forearms and elbows as you're doing many of the exercises, which means they'll develop along with the rest of your body. If you're still worried about it, get hold of a grip strength developer or do some rock climbing. They'll really do the trick.

How will I know if I'm overdoing it?

As long as you follow the two golden rules on page 35, you should be fine. Some muscle soreness is perfectly normal after training, but you shouldn't feel crippled. Slow, steady, regular process is the way forward. And remember to stretch.

Is there any one best time of day to train?

Different people work better at different times of day, so try shifting your workout around to see if it makes any difference. But most people can get used to training at any time, and derive exactly the same benefit from it.

Do I need to do any extra training for my back and shoulder muscles?

Good question. You often see guys in the gym with badly imbalanced musculature. The classic is the bloke who's spent too long on the bench, but has neglected his back, and has the hunched-forward shoulders to prove it. Not a good look. The principle I always bear in mind is 'just because you can't see it doesn't mean you don't have to work it'. But – to answer your question – no, you don't. The beauty of these two routines is that, followed correctly, they work all your upper body muscles. So there's no need for you to start doing separate exercises for your back and shoulders.

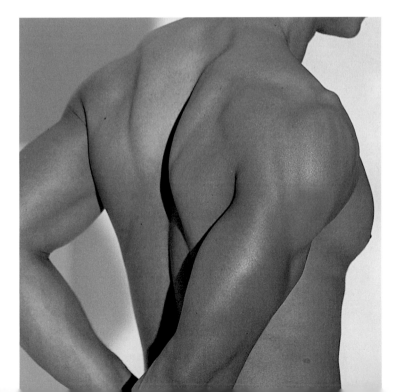

workout two

To be alternated with workout one, the 'pull' routine focuses on the muscles of your upper back and biceps.

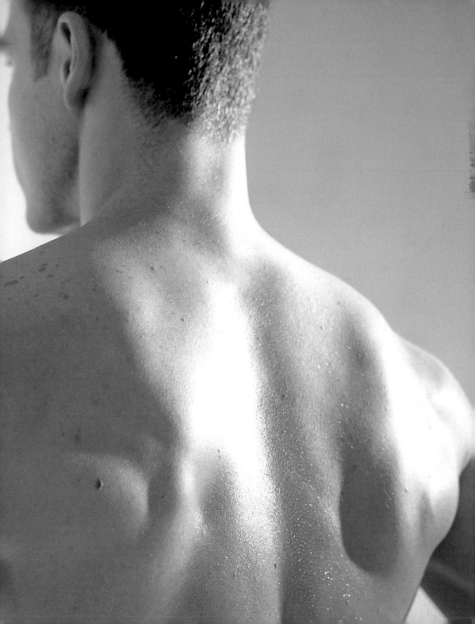

cardio

warm-up

To prime your muscles for the work to come, you need to warm up on a piece of CV kit for 5–10 minutes, just as you did before workout one. Again, you're not looking to kill yourself here, but to start raising a sweat. Use the rower or cross-trainer, as you prefer.

on the cross-trainer

If you're warming up on the cross-trainer, set the machine to a reasonably tough setting so that you have to work hard to push and pull. A stroke rate of about 120–140 strokes per minute is ideal. And make sure you work your arms as hard as your legs – it's easy to let them coast.

close pull-up

Definitely for when you're fresh. This is a real test for your lats (the fan of muscles at the side of your back). Do three sets of 10 reps on a pull-up bar or machine. Rests are 90 seconds.

1 With hands shoulder-width apart, hold the bar with palms facing behind you. Bend your knees and keep your feet together (to stop you swinging about).

2 Pull yourself up until your eyes are level with the bar. Keep your body as straight as possible. Hold for 1 second, then slowly lower yourself to the starting position.

If the close pull-up gives you gyp, turn to page 57 for my performance-improving tips

lat pull-down

This is the kneeling-down version of a classic gym exercise. Do it on the cable machine, or perform it sitting at a lat pull-down machine. It works your lats and rhomboids (the muscles between your shoulder blades) to perfection. Do three sets of 20 reps, dropping the weight by 20% with each set. Rests are 45 seconds.

1 Kneel at the cable machine and place your hands shoulder-width apart on the bar. Keep your back straight and your abs tight.

2 Grip the bar firmly and pull it down, breathing out as you do so. Watch you don't lean back. Slowly return to the start position, breathing in at the same time.

the close pull-up

The close pull-up on page 55 is tough. In fact, a significant percentage of men find it impossible to do even one. Here's a technique I recommend to anyone who can do them, but who can't do as many as they'd like. Do as many pull-ups as you can. When you've reached failure, place a bench or step under the bar. Hold the bar with the same grip, then jump up so that your chin is just above it. Now lower yourself with a slow, controlled movement. Go for failure again (you won't manage too many reps as you're really just tipping your muscles over the edge).

row

A great exercise for toning your biceps and the muscles of your upper back. To get the most from it, keep your legs and torso stock-still. Work on three sets (6 reps, 8 reps, then as many as you can). Rests are 45 seconds.

1 Sit facing the cable machine with your legs out in front of you and your knees slightly bent. Grip the bar with both hands.

back straight throughout

2 Pull the bar in close to your body, aiming for your lower chest. Hold for 1 second, then slowly return to the start, keeping your elbows tucked in tight.

shoulders square

supplements

Are there any natural alternatives to steroids?

When you look through fitness and bodybuilding magazines, you see all sorts of advertisements for fat-reducers, muscle-builders, and performance-enhancers, all of them purporting to be 'natural', 'safe', and 'legal'. At best, these are unproven, non-effective cons. At worst, they're extremely dangerous and harmful drugs. My advice is to go nowhere near them. There are no short cuts to success: hard muscle is gained by hard training; not by pills and potions.

I've read that creatine can help you pack on muscle. Is this true?

It's a common misconception that creatine causes muscle growth directly. Most of the initial 'lean gains' are actually due to increased muscle hydration. What creatine does do is allow you to lift heavier and train harder. But do ask yourself whether you really need it. Are you training as hard as you can without it? Have you achieved the maximum gains you can? Creatine doesn't work by magic; you still have to put the work in. It's also a relatively new product, and, as such, studies into the effects of its long-term use have not been possible. Only when this data comes in can creatine truly be assessed as safe.

I seem to have reached a plateau with my muscle-building and am considering taking protein powders and meal replacements. What do you think?

I think you don't need them (for the reasons I've mentioned on the opposite page). Follow the nutritional advice I've given you elsewhere in the book – particularly with regard to the quantity and quality of your protein intake – and keep on training hard, steadily increasing the number of reps you're doing and the weights you're lifting. And double-check that your goals are realistic. You will eventually reach your genetically set limit, but very few people do. It takes years of training to get to that point, not just a few months.

I get pretty discouraged when I look at some of the guys in bodybuilding magazines. Will I ever be able to get that big?

The answer is no, you probably won't, unless you take steroids. You can't build muscles that size without them. But it isn't worth the risk.

row

An exercise that builds big biceps and shoulders. Find a weight you can just manage 6 reps with. Drop the weight slightly, and aim for 8 more. Drop the weight again and push out as many as you can. Rests are 90–120 seconds.

1 Using an overhand grip, grab the bar firmly with both hands and hold it against your thighs.

2 Leading with your elbows, pull the bar up to the top of your chest. Keep it as close to your body as you can and watch you don't arch your back. Slowly lower it to the start position.

abs pulled in tight

pull-down

More work for your upper back and triceps. Aim for 10 reps for the first set. Drop the weight for the second and third sets and aim for 12 reps and 15 reps respectively. Rests are 90–120 seconds.

1 With your back straight and arms almost fully extended, grab the bar with an overhand grip.

2 Keeping your arms almost straight, slowly pull the bar down to waist level. Slowly return to the start position.

how much protein

Your daily intake of protein when you're strength training should be about 1.4g per 1kg of body weight (see below for imperial conversions). So, a 90kg man requires 126g of protein a day (1.4 x 90 = 126). When you consider that a single tin of tuna gives you 50g (2oz), this is not actually that much. But there's no point in eating any more – it simply goes down the loo.

in pounds and ounces

You need ¼oz of protein per 10lb bodyweight. So, a 200lb guy needs 5oz (20 x ¼).

arm row

An effective exercise that works your biceps, the backs of your shoulders, and your upper back. Use the same set/rep/rest routine as you used for the upright row on page 62.

back straight

1 Rest your left hand and left knee on the bench. Keep your right foot on the floor and hold the weight in your right hand. Keep your back straight.

2 Pull the weight towards your chest, keeping your body stable and your arm in close to your body. Return to the start, keeping the movement slow and controlled. When you've done all the reps with one arm, switch to the other and repeat.

arm in close to your body

There will be moments when it feels as if your arms are about to explode. Don't be put off – the sensation soon wears off. Besides, it means your hard work's paying off and you're building larger, stronger muscles.

bicep curl

A classic exercise. Find a weight you can just manage 15 reps with. Stay with it for a second and a third set and don't worry if you can manage only 8–12 reps. Rests are 60 seconds.

1 With feet hip-width apart and knees slightly bent, take your bodyweight through your heels. Place your hands at the sides of your thighs and hold the bar with an underhand grip. Keep shoulders relaxed and elbows tucked in.

keep elbows
tucked in tight

2 Keeping your elbows tucked in tight, bring your hands up until your forearms almost touch your biceps. Hold for 1 second, flex your biceps, then slowly return to the start.

rear delt fly

Great for strengthening the back of your shoulders and the muscles of your middle back. Use the same set/rep/rest routine as for the last exercise.

1 Stand with your knees bent and feet shoulder-width apart, the weight of your body on your heels. Lower your chest and stick your bottom out. Hold the weights with your arms slightly bent.

palms facing each other

2 Keeping your body still and your back straight, raise your arms to the sides, taking them as far back as you can. Hold the position for 1 second, then slowly return to the start.

back straight

eat big

how much carbohydrate

An essential part of bulking up is plentiful amounts of quality unrefined carbohydrates. In fact, round 60% of your calorie intake should be carbs. So, for a man eating 3000 calories a day, that's about 450g (1lb) of carbohydrate. Just in case you need the equation: 0.6 x 3000kcals = 1800kcals; each gram of carbohydrate = 4kcals, so 1800kcals divided by 4 = 450g. The figures are different in pounds and ounces, but the answer's the same: 1lb.

preacher curl

Your gym may well have a preacher curl bench, but no worries if it hasn't: you can mock it up as I did here. Use the same set/rep/rest routine as for the last two exercises.

1 Raise the bench to about 75°. Squat end-on to it with your back straight and upper chest resting against the pad. Rest your arm on the bench. Hold the weight with an underhand grip and rest your other hand on your thigh as support.

2 Raise your forearm and bring your wrist as close to your shoulder as you can. Slowly return to the start. When you've done all the reps with one arm, switch arms and repeat.

routine checkup

Do I need to incorporate cardio work into my muscle-building routine?

From a health and general fitness perspective, you definitely should. Bodybuilders are not as a rule 'fit and healthy' human beings, so aim to fit in three 20–30 minute bouts per week. If you're already quite a big guy, you may want to give running a miss and opt for a lower-impact activity. Swimming and cycling are fine, but I'd particularly recommend rowing – it's non-impact and has a fairly large strength component for an aerobic activity. Whatever kind of cardio work you go for, keep an eye on your body fat/lean tissue level to ensure you're not doing too much (and preventing muscle growth) or too little (and getting lardy).

I see other guys going into the gym with bottles of water. Should I be doing the same?

Most definitely. In fact, you shouldn't even think about stepping foot inside the gym without a bottle that holds at least a litre (1¾ pints). Water's essential for topping up your body's fluid levels, including the large amounts depleted from your muscles during exercise. Drink too little of the stuff and a process called acidic build-up can set in, causing stiffness and soreness. So always go well-supplied. Tap water's fine, but keep clear of the carbonated kind.

I'm keen to develop my upper body but really don't want to end up with a neck like a bulldog. How can I avoid it?

The muscles that run from the top of the neck across the top of the back and shoulders do develop very quickly in some guys, and it's this that gives them the bulldog look you talk about. You do have to work these trapezius muscles a bit, however. But, with the exercises in this book, you'll never overemphasize them.

concentration curl

Now – to polish off your biceps – a 'strip set'. Pick up a weight you can do 10 reps with, then pump out as many reps as you can. When you fail, drop the weight (no rest). Keep dropping the weight until you fail with even the smallest weight.

1 Grip the weight in one hand. Lean forward, resting your working arm against your inner thigh.

2 Raise the weight until it's almost at shoulder height, then slowly lower it to the starting position. Keep your back and legs still throughout. When you've reached failure with one arm, switch to the other arm.

half pull-up

This exercise should finish your muscles off completely. Do three sets of as many half pull-ups as you can, with a 30-second break between sets.

hands slightly wider than shoulder-width apart

1 Sit on the end of the bench, then grab the bar with an underhand grip that's slightly wider than shoulder-width apart. Keep your body straight, knees slightly bent and heels on the floor.

2 Keeping your body straight and supporting yourself on your heels, pull yourself up until your chest meets the bar. Slowly return to the start position.

body straight

stretches

To round off the workout, do the same stretches you did at the end of the first routine. Stretch your tightest or weakest side first. And take it good and slowly – this is time spent wisely.

1 chest stretch

Stand with feet hip-width apart. Hold your abs tight, but relax your head, neck, and shoulders. Keeping your back straight, clasp your hands behind you and lift your arms until you feel a stretch across your chest. Hold for 10–15 seconds.

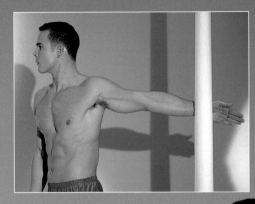

2 bicep and chest stretch

Stand at arm's length from a pole or wall with the palm of your hand resting against it. Keeping your arm straight, gently rotate your body away from your hand so you feel the stretch in your chest and arm. Hold for 15 seconds, then repeat with your other arm.

3 upper back stretch

Stand at arm's length from a pole, feet hip-width apart. Extend your arms in front of you and clasp the pole, lowering your head as you do so. Keep your lower back firm and your torso upright. Hold for 10 seconds.

4 tricep stretch

Stand with your feet hip-width apart. Raise one arm and place the hand over your back as if you were reaching down your spine. Gently push the elbow back with your other hand. Hold for 10 seconds, then repeat with your other arm.

5 shoulder stretch

Stand with your feet hip-width apart. Bend one arm slightly and stretch it across your body. Place your other hand on the upper arm to push the stretch a little further. Feel it in the back of your shoulder. Hold for 10 seconds, then repeat with your other arm.

7 neck stretch

Sit upright with shoulders relaxed. Cradle your head with one hand and gently pull it towards your shoulder. Feel the stretch at the side of your neck. Hold for 10 seconds, then repeat with your other hand.

6 forearm stretch

Sit or stand up straight. Extend one arm in front of you, elbow straight, palm facing forwards. Gently pull the fingers back with your other hand. Feel the stretch in your forearm. Hold for 10 seconds, then repeat with your other hand.

keeping it up

What's the best way to maintain muscle once I've put it on?

Just keep on training.. It's pretty tricky laying down hard and fast rules about this because eveyone's different. But – in general terms – two sessions a week should keep your muscles stimulated. Remember, though, that if you train less often than this you'll be burning fewer calories: best to drop your food intake or you could easily start to gain fat and lose definition.

I've started workout programmes before, but always end up throwing in the towel after a couple of weeks. What's the secret to keeping my motivation up?

To get the most from any training programme, it's important to keep on challenging your body. Recording the progress you're making at this can help you keep on track *and* keep motivated. It also highlights your strengths and makes you aware of any areas that need extra work. With these ends in mind, I've given you a training log to fill in for each workout on pages 88–91. At the end of each session, simply jot down the number of reps you did and how much you lifted. You'll then be able to see at a glance the improvement you're making. Good luck with it.

training log

Writing up a training log at the end of each session helps you keep track of your progress. It's also an efficient way of motivating yourself. As well as how many reps you did, and the weight you lifted (where relevant), note anything in particular you felt, such as totally ruined or on a high! Take photocopies of these pages so you have more sheets to fill in.

exercise	date weight / reps	date weight / reps	date weight / reps
medicine ball throw			
set 1	– / 20	– / 20	– / 20
set 2	– / 20	– / 20	– / 20
set 3	– / 20	– / 20	– / 20
flat bench press			
set 1	/	/	/
set 2	/	/	/
set 3	/	/	/
incline press			
set 1	/	/	/
set 2	/	/	/
set 3	/	/	/
dumbbell press			
set 1	/	/	/
set 2	/	/	/
set 3	/	/	/

exercise	date weight / reps	date weight / reps	date weight / reps
pec fly			
set 1	/	/	/
set 2	/	/	/
set 3	/	/	/
side raise			
set 1	/	/	/
set 2	/	/	/
set 3	/	/	/
french press			
set 1	/	/	/
set 2	/	/	/
set 3	/	/	/
front raise			
set 1	/	/	/
set 2	/	/	/
set 3	/	/	/
classic press-up			
set 1	– /	– /	– /
set 2	– /	– /	– /
set 3	– /	– /	– /
triceps bench dip			
set 1	– /	– /	– /
set 2	– /	– /	– /
set 3	– /	– /	– /

training log

exercise	date weight / reps	date weight / reps	date weight / reps
close pull-up			
set 1	– /	– /	– /
set 2	– /	– /	– /
set 3	– /	– /	– /
lat pull-down			
set 1	/	/	/
set 2	/	/	/
set 3	/	/	/
seated row			
set 1	/	/	/
set 2	/	/	/
set 3	/	/	/
upright row			
set 1	/	/	/
set 2	/	/	/
set 3	/	/	/
pull-down			
set 1	/	/	/
set 2	/	/	/
set 3	/	/	/
single arm row			
set 1	/	/	/
set 2	/	/	/
set 3	/	/	/

exercise	date weight / reps	date weight / reps	date weight / reps
barbell bicep curl			
set 1	/	/	/
set 2	/	/	/
set 3	/	/	/
rear delt fly			
set 1	/	/	/
set 2	/	/	/
set 3	/	/	/
classic preacher curl			
set 1	/	/	/
set 2	/	/	/
set 3	/	/	/
concentration curl			
set 1	/	/	/
set 2	/	/	/
set 3	/	/	/
set 4 (if done)	/	/	/
set 5 (if done)	/	/	/
half pull-up			
set 1	– /	– /	– /
set 2	– /	– /	– /
set 3	– /	– /	– /
notes			

information

working out at home

There will be days when you won't have the time to go to the gym but are still keen to work out. There'll be other occasions when you simply want to top up your routine from the day before. Home gym equipment is the answer.

setting up a home gym

These days you can buy several pieces of inexpensive, easy-to-store home gym equipment that mean you can train a good range of muscle groups and achieve an excellent overall workout. Simplicity is the key: the more complicated the kit is to use or maintain, the more unlikely it is you'll ever make use of it.

dumbbells

The dumbbells on sale for home use are pretty similar to those you find in the gym. The only significant difference is that the gym probably has a far greater choice. Before you rush off to the shops, analyse your workout routines to determine the range of weights you use most. Then choose a range of around five pairs of dumbbells – start with a weight that's suitable for the final set of an exercise like the concentration curl and go up to the maximum you'd use for an exercise like the pec fly. Adjustable dumbbells might seem like a more economical buy than a set, but continually stopping to change weights will greatly reduce the effectiveness of your training. Besides a good set of one-piece dumbbells should last a lifetime. And you can always buy heavier dumbbells gradually as your strength increases.

bar and weights

A single 6–7ft bar and a basic set of weights shouldn't cost the earth. Again, analyse your routines to find out which you need. I'd suggest a couple of 2.5kg (5lb) weights, four 5kg (10lb) weights, and two 10kg (25lb) weights. Don't forget to get a pair of collars too, but save the squat stands until you're feeling flush – you can always make do with the rack on the bench (*see below*).

exercise bench

Go for one that has a rack. That way, you never need worry about having someone there to spot for you. Make sure it's sturdy enough *and* high enough.

medicine balls

Not the most obvious choice for a piece of domestic exercise equipment, but the medicine ball has uses in the home training programme beyond the medicine ball throw. It's particularly good for ab work, where it intensifies the work in crunches and squats. Choose either a 3kg (6lb) or 5kg (11lb) ball.

The only other piece of equipment you might think about getting is a full-length mirror so you can keep a close eye on yourself.

index

credits

author's credits

Thanks to everybody (too many of you to name, alas) who helped me with this book. A special thank you to the DK team, to Michael, Tracy, and Anna, in particular; to Russell for the great shots; to my own team, especially Nik, Richard, Jason, Ayo, and Alan; and to my brother Jon, who, as always, shared the workload with me. For more information about Matt Roberts Personal Training, please contact:

matt roberts personal training
32–34 Jermyn St
London SW1Y 6HS
Tel: 020 7439 8800
www.personaltrainer.uk.com

publisher's credits

Special thanks to Nik Cook for his invaluable expert help and advice. Thanks also to our models Jon Firth and Lee Stafford from ModelPlan, and to Nessie at ModelPlan; to Matt's team of trainers: George Dick, Jason Hughes, Ayo Williams, and Alan Foley; to Toko at Hers for hair and make-up; to stylist Jo Atkins-Hughes; to photography assistant Nina Duncan; and to designer Janis Utton. Many thanks to Reebok for the kind loan of trainers for this book (all enquiries 0800 30 50 50).

about the author

Matt Roberts, the UK's hottest personal trainer, began as an international sprinter. He went on to complete his studies at the American Council for Exercise and the American College of Sports Medicine. Affectionately known as 'the personal trainer to the stars', Matt has an enviable reputation for training celebrities, among them Sandra Bullock, Trudie Styler, Mel C, Natalie Imbruglia, Naomi Campbell, Tom Ford, John Galliano, and Faye Dunaway. Alongside this high-profile client list, Matt derives equal satisfaction from helping each of his clients meet their health and fitness goals. And in his quest to make fitness and good health accessible to everyone, he produces his own range of vitamins, home gym equipment, and body care products.